1

I'd rather be damned by my honesty,
than bound by my lies.

Gothic Inferno: The Beast Within

13th Anniversary Edition

Omega Maverick

{ The Everlasting Unleashment
of a Soul's Gentle Tune }

I find sorrow.
This lake has taken my true love.
We had frolicked and we had laughed.
We thought of the next day...
We believed there would be more days.

But it took her.
She was rendered ashes
upon the lake of sorrow.

I gaze blankly upon the lake.
I ponder the gentle lapping
upon the shore.

It makes me want to be...
Coupled with her in time's caress.

To visit her blissful corpse.
Hear her laughing in aquatic splash.
A taken love; her corpse still resting.

Somewhere...

Beneath those rounded ripples.

{ Eyes on Venice }

Life is here,
the time is now.
The milk for cheese comes from the cow.
But it must age,
as so must we...
So that we may keep climbing
up life's rough tree.

Hands together and hands apart;
so far away but
always close to my heart.

Eyes on Venice,
hearts that Rome,
Where is it that
anyone truly calls home...

Spoiled, rotten,
cheese is mold...

A tale to tell of broken hearts.
Penicillin gives a healing start.
Even when hearts still bleed.

So do not protest,
it shall be in vein.
For the healing has come;
wasting medicine would be a shame.

{ The Valley of Skin }

I walk the valley of skin.

Looking in the eyes of strangers.
Seeing the stranger I am.

I walk in silence.
Begging someone to listen.

Screaming to ears.
Deaf ears.

Looking to the horizon.
I see nothing.

{ Gazers }

Gazers...

Broken at night.
Draining from the eyes.
Coagulated shit drips.
Tasting death's caress.

{ Pen Driven Sword }

Ever gone. Never Free.
Why do you not wait for me?

Hold on tight!
Just let go...

Never enough time.
Relax, enjoy the show.

Enough then more.
Just too good.
Everyone left misunderstood.

Never alone in the world of sheep.
Who the hell am I? Little Bo Peep?
Everything stands when nothing falls.
Follow a crowd sitting in stalls.

Keep slaving away.
Help starving children.
Just pennies a day.

Your children are wasting away.

Why look at the eyes of tomorrow?
When yesterday's lies just left sorrow.

Always is good. Never is better.
Every sharp pain. Life carving you.

Word after word written on your chest.
By pen-driven sword beneath your
breast.

{ Dark Jaded Eyes }

Water eyes sand storm.
Reality's grip slowly slips.
Hands do rumble.
Breath gasps to pray.
Mind race dreams.
Riding, mares of the night.

Your presence among fragments.
So glad you misunderstood.

Feeling new soul dawn.

So, come. now.
As we begin to cry.

Let one last twinkle glimmer.
Forever in these dark jaded eyes.

{ Inferno of Tears }

Into the arms of death come I.

I, black waters of confusion.
I, hands of bottomless wrath.
I, bombed beach of sanity.

It infects me.
It infests me.

I, must maim.
I, lack mercy to kill.

Burn it all down.
Before it crumbles.

I, disintegrate.
I, melted by my inferno of tears.

{ Waterfall of Apes }

The apes fall down.
Cascading waterfall.
Whimsically tumbling down.
To death!

Creatures, lemmings.
Desperately Clasp.
To branches. To twigs.
No support.

snap-break-snap-snap

See the sun!
Before plummeting.
Pray to it...

Death gears grind.
Minimal disruptions.

{ I Love You }

Gone but never from my heart.
Only wish: your happiness.

Love is always here

Never lost.
Only sights changed.
However: This. Never. Will.

I will always love you.

A new heart holds your hand.
To neither shatter nor maul.

Never to do what I did.
Never at all.

But, know this to be true.

I still so very much love you

{ Too Many Too Few }

I tread this valley.
Feces fecal faces silent stare.

Shit hidden inside truth.
Find the none in many.

Too many too few.
All of them broken.

It's time to fix it... **BOOM.**

{ War of Reality }

Slicing. Dicing.
Holding court.
Standing stalwart in my fort.

Golden chalice.
Breaking bread.
Soon enough you'll be dead.

Shaking Hands.
Scuffling Feet.
In war meat talks to meat.

Impossible hopes meet scuffed dreams.
Forests are burned.
Dirtied are the streams.

Shame and regret.
No further to get.
Reality still further yet.

Shuddering in a room.
Impending gloom.
Too many sounds in this tomb.

{ Smell Your Hunger }

I smell your hunger.
Passion fills the air.

Your passion turns on you.

A smile fills your eyes.
Subtle thoughts making hips move.
Finding the chink in your armor.

I slide in.

You know your caught.
But you don't mind.
You knew it was inevitable.

If given time.

{ Eternal Peace }

Woes and thrills.
Ingest these bitter pills.

Just a touch of death please.
Life's a thrill.

Eyes downcast.
Heartbeat still.

Death's no release.
There is no eternal peace.

{ Bath Time }

Blood filled veins.
Dripping down flesh.
Primal mechanism activation.

Blood pumps faster.
Desire replies.
Eagerness, a soul's invitation.

Blood drains over my face.
Slowly encasing.

Bath of life juice.
Struggles entombing.

will to live.
Writhing, coagulating.

Heart beats last shudder.

A heart was alive.
But, the view was askew.

{ Rules of the Game }

Athletes and Gods

Rules of the game.
Book to Book.

They are the same.

Kneel down and prey.
Non-believer.
Sinners and saints.

Your team the devil.
Winning team the faith.

Sportscaster/Preacher

Let them through the gates.

{ The Valley of the Lost Child }

Walking the valley.
Searching the fields.
Never finding that which was promised.

Heart beats loudly.

Just wanting the dark prince to take
her away.

To...

A new place.
A little peace.
One more day.

The lost child appears then fades away.
Looking for brighter days.
One free moment.

Still she is lost.
Ever so lost...

In the valley of the lost child.

Sadly...
Ever so sadly,
I must move on.

More valleys ahead...

{ Friends Close But... }

Enemies keep the boundary lines
drawn well.

But, keep guard.

Friends are the real danger.
With them one can never tell...

{ Beats Silent }

Light dimming as air grows cold.
All too late.
You've grown old.

Heartbeat burns.
Scars do last.
Soon enough.
Beats silent.

No hurry.
Your life.

  Devour it.
     Savor it.
      Love it.
     Live it.

When you don't.
Someone else will.

No regrets.

Get your fill,
or be left to starve.

{ Empty Prison Cell }

Soiled clothes do rot.
Scalding, folding, bought.
Washing, trying, clean.
Life's marring unseen.

Wish better days.
Thoughts coming gaze.
Now just a haze.

Neutered, muted, wrong.
Life's sullen song.
Something gone long.

Sitting in the stalls.
Breathing in the faults.

Falling broken bones.
Slithered withered tones.

Echoing in this...
Empty prison cell.

{ Googolplex of Curves }

Lurking in night.
Wonder after satin.
Shall she come.

Look inside closed windows.
Beautiful skin light.
Infinite googolplex of curves.

Bringing erection remorse.

I want to dance.
I want to die.
I want to live each moment...

As if it were our first.

Loving hate heart.
I wonder, 'is it cursed?'

Peeking at the window of her soul.
Pondering if she'll cry...

{ Clouded by the Sun }

Walk in figures.
Entranced by lies.
Encased in darkness.
Shiver in the light.

Fire from the bowels.
Coming through mangled plain.
Salvation of a withered soul.

Corpse walks through existence.
Floating suit. Gray eyes.
Fettered like bee to the hive.

Only ravaged substance.
Decay encased withered mind.
Revives a laugh.
Frozen by the coldness of time.

Away shall you go.
Clouded by the sun.
Never read the lore!

Energized corpse.
Electric forced life.
Blood light touches.

FIGHT!
Fight!
fight...

{ The Softest Caress }

The river changes you.
Currents estrange.
Movement pains.
Someone unchains you.

Paddling murky waters.
Mind's eye crackle.
Mud stains spackle.

Serenading cries.
Treading lies.
Falls beneath.

Death: The Softest Caress

{ Make You Cry }

Golden lies

Between a million oh's and sigh's.
Different, not worth their time.
Is it right for them, to make you cry?
Is it now your time to die?

Everyone wants your soul.
Give into control.
Your creativity; they stole.

Little boxes.
Numbered lines.
Too many words.
Not so kind.

Forget them.
Their ways.
Numb days.

Hold on to your mind.
Every moment of pain.

Your death is on the way.
Live for today.
Do they care if you decay?

{ Bitter Dust }

Eyes opened by dark times.
Too many riddles given.

Words of those came before.
They loved you... they said.

Lasting love; quick cold lust?

Heart's bitter dust.
Loathing days... one to the next.

Bloodied meat puppet...
Sewn back together?

Warmed against my chest.
Will you go, like all the rest?

I can only be my best...

{ Is This Misfortune? }

Spinning across gray shadows.
Night spills forth comforting darkness.
Tempts to see a taste of it.
Indulgent innocent intentions.

Want to play?

Darkness: Embrace It.
Soon engulfed.
Merged with it violently.
Vengeance power... submerged.

Is this misfortune?

Transformation's spun web.
Keep safe the silver cord.
Radiance inside embraced.
Darkness overcomes sadness.

How to see again?

Power to entrance entities.
Darkness and light.
Dancing brilliant glow.
Followed behind it...

Cannot comprehend the potential?

Reality's combination.
Elements positive and negative.
Lightly shrouded by gloom.
Happiness reflection of
unfolded events.

Do you see the balance?

{ Embittered Heart }

Hearts meeting fast.
Aching for this to last.

Is it real or another fake?

Another bucket of bitterness.
Poured into this lake.
Realize please...

A heart is at stake.

Another stake through soul.
Just cruel jest uncontrolled.
One mere moment hidden from shame.
Last breath by an embittered heart.

Another beginnings end?

Another false start.
In the eyes words that scream.
"Is it ashes or candy?"
Watch your speeches.

Soul hollowed out again and again.

A has been could have been reality?
A chance begged reality?
Crush me cruel deceit!
Wait and wonder whilst heart skips
a beat.

No reality when souls do meet?

{ A Valley of Shadow }

Walking a valley of shadow.
Burning land of pain.
Writing through the sun.

I, the invisible.
Walking through crowds.
Seeing empty faces.

No name badges.
No friendship.
No camaraderie.

Wading through the dense throng.

Hold me tight confusion.
Sing to masses deaf ears.
Make peace so violent.

Hands upon me.

Look at me!
Look in my direction!

Give unbelieving looks.
Give me the disgust.

Response, action, attention.
Anything will do!

Scream to the masses.
No one will listen.

Go to the mountains.

Lobby the heavens.
Asking Gods, 'why?'

I see them...
looking down at me.
I see them...
laughing at me.

Telling me.

"You. Yes, you are the reason."
"Who do you let in?"

Fools!

"You're scared."
"You're hurt."

Lies!

"You let the past be your world."
"Holding on tightly to failures."
"Look at your accomplishments."

Nothing... Nothing to see here.

Let's move on...

{ Watching the Beast }

Flight crash sunlight.
Begin night processional.

Evil all-showing light.

Wait at garden gate.
Watching the beast.

Driving the sun from west to east.

Still waiting.
Still debating.

Am I still hanging?
Am I already dead?

{ Speck of Light }

World of hate.
Words of scrrow.

Speck of light?
Truth: The rarest gift.

Quest always far.
Grasp away the questions.

Within one mind.
No true way.

Lies to obtain.
Life's sad refrain.

{ A Harsh Place }

Please show me harm.
Pain sorrow sustenance.

Hungering for more.
Longing to be the fool.

A harsh place.
A true place.
A place calls to me.

A place I should stay to break free.

{ By The End... }

Drones in the obscure night.
Soul's reasoning lost.

Shades of blacks to blues.
Crawling into their beds.

Soil soon covering heads.
Silent nocturnal sails.

Laying in wait for days to come.

Realizing by the end...
I am numb.

{ Field Mouse Running }

Flying in the night.
Eyes set: run!
Heart beat ever faster.
Sore gracefully.

One more chase.
Swoop down.

Run swiftly.
Days gone bye.
New world found.

Others... her kind.
Exist.

Still high above the clouds.
Poised to strike.

So she ran...

Plucked from the ground.
One then another.

Always, wondering...

If she'd never recover.

{ 64000/20 ~ 1 }

Image whispering.
Echoes of mind lies.
Different outcome from gallery inside.

Incandescent shame shines.
Prolonging... your... aching...

Rotting and commanding.
Illuminate fields of understanding!

A jealous heart escapes, away.

Still shackled.
Withered cage.

Built by hidden veils.
Feeding pockmarked heart,
ancient fairy tales.

Sold to Prince Harming.
Longing to believe.

Subtle fables.
Opaque lies.

Vision is 64000/20.
If you're looking for approval.

Deaf ears may hear.
Never giving way to understanding.

Eye doors closed to stagnation.
Grazing at brick lace religion.

A soul's gentle lust.
No tender touch.

Porcelain gods inside.
Spirits do rust.

Bitterness alone.
Forged. Drugged out...

Sewn eyes satiated.
If only they masturbated...

Drugs calm interrogated.

Cold haven.
Drug-laden.
Hide-away from home.

No easy voices.
Patiently aching for release.

Doorways to happy tomorrows.
Doomed to premature termination.

Time pieces turn back.
Feces locked.
Missing keys.

Lying time never works.

Deceased morals.
Only mortals can shatter.

The Glass Prison.

{ Patience }

That thing we get after banging our
heads into the wall.

One.

Too.

Many Times.

{ The Immortal Mirror }

Eyes in the immortal mirror.
Things I's do fear.
Breath clouds the image.

Staring for hours; hoping for change.
Hating visions from day to day.

Listening to whispers in your head.
Hoping soon they'll be dead
Holding tight to glistening light.

Gazing at cries of tomorrow.
Overwhelmed...
Apprehension; fright.

Wasting away is an awful sight.
Fearing too much of becoming the light.
Aching for dreams that you will die.

Seeing no tears left behind.
Wishing to not want to go.
Finally frayed so long ago.

No more days.
Blinding light, go away!
Clawing deep into this lost soul.

Decay cost all.
Never swayed.
Fear no further days.

Pining for a caress of cold edge.
Strawberry splatters draining meal.

But, wait!

When its draining away...

Just wishing for another day.

{ Satiate The Nomad }

Wildflowers in your eyes.
Raindrops from the heart.
Prism doorway to our souls.

Entity takes flight.
Beyond scabs & scars tortures untold.

Burned skin pathway of pain.
Wandering through life.

Wanton for days.
Better ways.
Different places.
Golden grays.

Gypsy heart; seeded by soul.
New air breath. Unable to control.

Anywhere fresh air.
People estranged.
Without a care.

Quest not destination.
Wandering these same streets.

Roads? Highways?

Satiate the nomad.
Stealing bright skies.
Mesmerizing hum.

Engine takes you away.

Off to another day.
Another air in the middle of nowhere.
Look into the sky.

Simply, wanting to share.

{ Dear Sir }

How ghastly was your thought
last night, kind sir?

Did it cause fear or pleasure,
kind sir?

Could you kill with delight
tonight, kind sir?

Does your mind or furrowed brow,
bring you to the here and now,
kind sir?

Have you reveled in her pain,
kind sir?

What is the essence of your darkness,
dear sir?

Do you laugh in the face of earthen
playthings,
kind sir?

Is your mind near or far,
kind sir?

If she gave you the mind inside her,
would you wish her suffering near dead,
kind sir?

If she isn't faithful to you?
If she doesn't show you respect?
That only you feel you deserve...

Will you hit her,
dear sir?

Are you everything you wanted?
Do you see you in the mirror?
Can you, do you, ever hear her,
kind sir?

Was there anything you could do?

Anything you could have given,
to help her live?

Sir, would you have said the things you
said, kind sir?

After all is said and done.
After all the wishes are wished.
After all the games are won.

Will you still love her, kind sir?
Will you show it?
Will you, dear sir?

{ The Valley of Harbored Emotions }

Off to a valley of harbored emotions,
seeing pale face doll stares.
Frozen, cracked, forgotten.

Rejectamenta.

Piles of refuse eagerly built.
Cherished then forgotten.
A figurine kin to me.

Abandoned souls just as mine.
Forgotten freaks of fortitude.
Loved then thrown to the incinerator.

There to amuse them
for a finite period.

Wanted no longer.
Used up.
Withered.

In haste dropped and cracked.
Once beautiful.
Marred beauty.

No longer caring.
No longer knowing.
Joy.

Rage builds.
Stigma makes me grow...
strong!

Building from what once was.
Growing for what may come.
A treasurer of lost souls.

Holder of secrets whispered in passion.
Keeper of dark hearts,
holding futures passed.

Always shaping better days.

{ Flaw in the Universe }

Mars against the wind.
Fighting children of daylight.
Looking down again.

Some time face shrouded.
Lust for life touted.
When force starts mounting.

Day breaks, head quakes.
How is it when knights collide?
Daylight's pride with an ache inside...

For anyone to cry.

Wishing for heart beat silence.
Stealthily end breath.
Binging on death's gaze.

Tearing quaking.
Our bond is breaking.
Waiting for last tremble.

Crimson washing free.
A flaw in the universe.
You and me.

{ The Breathing Dead }

Fires in the drain of life.

Nothing else to hope for.

See the grand scheme!

(too many overlook what is
different; the small.)

The breathing dead.
Totally forgotten.

Look to the stars...
A sky of ants playing at dusk.

Wondering what's worth saving...
Too many too few.
But, it will all pass without me.

My time came after I left.

Free from.
This body to the next.

The next life...
Will I read this writing I write?
Exclaiming...
This is mine!

...Only to be thought a fool...

The darkness surrounds me.
Tries to encompass me.
Holds me.
Fills me.

With dark love.

Life controlled by
the horrors of mediocrity.

Evils of the herd.
Pettiness controlling destiny.

Run from the herd!
Or... get trampled by it.

{ Make It Blind }

I spray putty!
I shoot paste!
I look outside... it's a disgrace.

Use, brutalize, and rape one blind.

For what?

So... they feel better at dinner time?
So... look at them with wide open eyes.

It is they whom they despise.

Injecting waste, filth, and muck.
Rape a soul and make it blind.

Now, please, break free and
kick ass this time.

{ This is My Fortress }

Fire flames.
Barbs of steel.
Barrier of glass.

A cube.
This cube.
Will this be my last?

Inner rage.
Slithering in spirit.
Restraints: rectangle or octagon?

This is my fortress.

A love of word in print.
A wish you find malevolent.
Inside this hidden cabin I have built.

Brought down by words
as they are spilt.

No longer to shock or amaze.
Spreading daze behind this haze.

No guard or beast keeps me here.
Only shivering alone.
Soaked in fear.

{ No Shelter for Angels ~ 2 }

Scarred eyes of rigid dogma.
Torn hands nails driven deep.

No shelter for angels.
Wings became shattered dream.

Angels sheltered tears.
Made of lies.

Inside that danger laced mortal face.
Powdered lines of white washed waste.

Tattered life spaces,
lived in fearful places.

Total disgraces.
All.

{ Harsh Realities }

Break into this prison.
Created for myself.

Force through walls.
Cremated memories.

Reinforced by iron.
Too many times to mention.

Harsh realities.

Making way into convalescent existence.
People walk by forcing decay.

Please, free me, from this hell...

{ The Valley of Rot & Plague }

The valley of rot and plague,
makes me hold my breath,
till light headed visions drain.

Eyes dead. Their words.
Transmissions garbled.

Rot and decay bring,
clean bright death.

Falling into a creeping light.

Must run!

Communicable mediocrity.
Their rot!
Their filth!

Look in to hallow eyes.
See empty shells!

Run from the plague!
Run!

{ Cutting Red Butter with a Cold Blue Knife }

One moment.
Ember becomes flame.

One second.
Match strike ignites.

One hour.
Pulse beats faster.

One sentence.
Can change a world.

One paragraph.
Illuminating.

One word.
Defies all reason.

One life.
Ethereal.

One day.
All it takes.

One heart.
To beat again.

{ Oath to Lord High Cheese }

I, worshiper of lord high cheese, of
the planet fermented moo milk, The
Edible Mold, or The Prince Of Dairy
products.

He is the child of cow and is brought
into this mooing world by the Bucket of
milk. Then his processing will come.

The farmer says,

"THEN THE COWS WILL DISTRIBUTE MORE
MILK, THE CHEESE WILL RISE FROM THE
DAIRY CASE WITH CREAMER AND OTHER DAIRY
PRODUCT BY IT'S SIDE IN THE
SUPERMARKET."

The CHEESE & Other Assorted dairy
products are no one but our lord high
milk's children with supreme commander
cheese.

So we've got to wait till the right
time and eat them.

{ The Book of Nothingness }

Stained and broken!
A welder reattaches my joints.
I am to be repaired.

Soon, walking down streets.
Why are there purple ducks
flying backwards?

Fields ahead, several men
grazing on grass.

To the dairy!
Women being milked from their udders.
Streams and green bears
swimming upstream.

Gazing rain-coated mountains.
Freeze or catch fire?

A horse being ridden by a car.
Hey, eggs are eating chickens.

Walk through a forest made of clay.
Trees and saplings
basking in the shade.

Toss a river into the stone...
Ripples in the stone!

Looking to the TV seeing humor.
Soon, riding...
silicone dildo trolley car.

Focusing on misconstrued conclusions.
Finding only disconcerting stillness.

Trying to fail yet succeeding to win.

Having a single word found in
the book of nothingness.

Bouncing freely on the birthday cake.
Walking back inside the down staircase.

Simply, finding a creature
looking up at me.

Somehow knowing...
everything is how it should be.

{ Blood, Cum, & Wasted Goods }

Blood on the floor.
Banging on the door!
Peer though the hole.

As it has been,
a million times before...

Breath beating past.
Staring at the parted grass.
Arched body moving fast.

Hearing her shriek!
Soon, curdling scream.
So soon seems sheik.

One cannot wait...
for it to get quiet.

For this day to be her last.

Wasting Away.
  Rotting, decay.
    Holding onto dreams.

Soon, her spirit frays.

Cleaning the blood.
  Seeing the dove.
    Want it to end.

Virginity is a sin.

Nothing left. Give up in the end.
  Just... blood, cum, & wasted goods.

{ No More Yesterdays }

Delicate hands of days roughed.

Holding close the rainbows;
effervescent beauty fizzles away.
Reflections etched upon the trees.

Doomed from light.
Still of night.
Soft breeze rattles the brush.

Hold on dreams.
Never knowing no more yesterdays.
The sway of green nestled breath.

Moonlight's prism.
Illuminates inner currency.

Morally bankrupt.

{ Wash Me Dirty }

Gasping.
Wishing.
Wanting.
Waiting.
Hoping: no hope.

Overflowing with rage.
Concentrating on hate.
Only to forget.
Concrete hate.
Overjoyed. To destroy!
Coagulating hate.

Fear feeding hate here.

Hate, please, washing me clean.
Hate, wash away the pain...
Relived on by forces unseen.

Whispered hate of hope.
Hate my friend to the end.
Hate wins once again.

Tear me down tears.
Foundation cracking?

Am I in the ground yet?

Hate thinking.
Loathing myself for breathing.

Believing...

Never seeing.
Needed seething.
Never knowing.

Overflowing with rage.
Concentrating on the hate.
Only to forget.
Concrete hate.
Overjoyed. To destroy!
Coagulating hate.

Washing me dirty today.

Hate eternal friend.
Hate at the beginning.
Rage till the end.

Hate bled tears.
Consecrate this body.
Hate myself beauty.

For wash me dirty eternity...

{ Premature Evacuation }

Reinventing myself.
Letting no one in.

Hating I for...
berating myself.

Inseminated with hate!
Washing away my youth.
Premature evacuation.

About to take my hate?
Everything I have worked for...
filth so deep & clean.

Eternal friend or enemy enema?
Rage from the beginning.
Will it be? There at the end?

Cries from within withered shell.
De-constructing my body.

Bleaching life's asshole.
Until there is only hate.

Till all is lost and...
I am simply skinless shit.

{ A Valley of Spirits }

Floating alone.
Dying to stand.
Command's supple breath.

Shining vacant eyes.
Wandering?
No gratitude...

Wondering through a valley of spirits.

Sullen dances & vicious romances.
Never really got they'd get scorned.
Bye lost life one may have worn.

A valley of spirits walked lightly.
Unsightly creatures.
Tread violent shores.
Tales of fists before.

Grass grows. Laid to rest.
Specter flies to valley end.
Done with the plains and valleys

Brain blown before final breath.
Spirit fluid. Spirit's unrest.

A lover's desires.
Pummeled.

Waking night scare.
Find a way out of unpleasant abode.
Made by lost souls.

All ways/Always | Scream. Lover.

Must keep walking...

Before this valley engulfs.
No getting left behind.

Just another spirit...
A specter in time.

{ Labels }

Not wanting labels is akin to,
cutting off your feet because they
itch.

You may alleviate the itch...

However, you won't be able to walk.

{ Decay Oppresses }

Once Flesh.
I stand rotten.

Beauty filth destroyed.
Decay oppresses.

Corpse mountain groans.
Turning dirt dead.
We will win.

Brethren.
Destroy.

Those.
Once.
Us.

{ A Gift that Keeps on Killing }

Matches to gasoline.
Words all burn.
Can't do a damn thing.

Before I explode!

Tearing across the tracks of life.
Bullet from a nun...

A thousand fears.
A million years.
Still no day of rest.

When will you believe?
When will you see?

Unbind heart attack pain.
Stoned dark heart.

The end is the beginning.
Now it is the time for rest.

Plunge a dagger through my breast.

Die forever.
Never forget.

Together for never.
No regret.

Time to burn.
Burnout. Match to death.
Sell the ashes?

Blow me away, today.
Bring me the wounded.

A gift that keeps on killing.

Joy curse attack.
No coming back?

What do you do with your death?
Now that only the struggle is left.

{ Laid in the Moment }

A look.
Your eyes.

Gazing up.
Begging.

Your motions, mine.
Tell me your stories.
Lies laid in the moment.

Bodies attuned to one purpose.
A universe rendered meaningless.

They.
Are.
Singularity.

Machine's ҫears pumping.

No beginning.
No end.

Finish/Start: Irrelevant.

Only movement matters now.

{ Stripped Permission }

Looking outside in.
Inside non-reflective mirror.

Hidden.

I see you...
Looking from the other side?

Do you mind!

I look...

We wait...

They listen.

Night's trembling glisten.
Heartbeat missing.

Life needs no permission.

To be stripped away.
To slip away.

Breathing memories.
Blissful memoirs.

Fade away.

{ Hue of Opaque ~ 3 }

Heed this warning.
Do not stay!

Fatal wounds.
Do not seek!

The plot is broken.
Six ruler sleep.

Write down date?
Carve it in blood.

Whittle away headstone.
You do make.

It is all gray...
A hue of opaque.

Always lose clock...
Heart is inside you.

Never displaced.
Despise you.

No fond company.
Infernal fucking clock!

Only a friend.
Once it sets you free.

{ The Valley of Men & Toys }

To the valley of men and toys.
Fools!
Squandering time's sacred fragments.

Unenjoyment ascertained,
abusements of amusements.

Cruelties. Cultivated.
Caustic words.

Scabs of brutality.
Subtleties of deconstruction.

Epidemic of anemic spirits
surrounds them.

Astounded by bitter withering weather.

Better to destroy enjoyments,
than to walk alone.

{ Who Cares..? Not. I. }

Tomorrow spits upon me.
Yesterday too much of the same.
Time, calls me names.

Looking past vision, rhyme,
violation, and lore.
Raped by reason's whore.

A number alone,
but, never given satisfaction.
Blasting the holier-than-thou.

Stand ahead.
None now behind.

Embrace dread.
Hate my kind.

Who cares..?

Not.
I.

{ Broken Rusted }

A relationship broken crusted.

Winter/Fall

Spring is rusted.
Gone, we trusted.

These gears weren't busted.
How did we become so crusted?

Broken rotten corpse,
of things before...

Tears dried the gears.
Re-broken heart is rusted.

Fall/Winter

From where did I spring?
Trusted, crusted, forever busted.

So pure.
So rusted.

Tried to mend,
machine fucking wrecked.

Truth found so feared.
I was the one... so broken rusted.

{ Muttered Pricks }

Mind holes.

Blackened souls.
Blackened soles.

Trampled down.
A beautiful rose.

Dark and decayed.
Browned violent thorn.

Lonely rose.
Darkened trap.

Form a defense!

Trampled petals.
Muttered pricks.

Passersby...

Too close.
Too close.

{ Rose Thorns }

Hard maybe soft.
Night's final tear...
Blood stained pillows.

Blanket held tight.
Soft tissue torn.

Mind heart ripped.
Rose thorn caresses.

Eyes are fury.
Mind of haze.

Nocturnal turns infernal.
Life's bitter ways.

Simple dance,
plight of souls asunder.

Belligerent release
Vs.
Intellectual aggression.

Always battling each other.

{ Love Me, Subtle Beast }

Requiring ache present.
Forfeiture, rape my soul.
Longing for a taste.
Dark entity executes need.
Hunger embitters me to them.
Loving the moment.
Razor-skinned pale.
Laughing at...

Your belief there is empathy.

Realization never shall arrive.

Subtle creatures vague,
borne of violation,
omnipotent flagellation,
of every little lamb.

Brings forth the animal that I am now.

Stolen ignorance to moments of sorrow.
Every little dream.
Gone. Withering. Tomorrows.
Spent before they came.
Life's careless novelties.

> Frightened creation encased.
> Within hard candy shell.
> Palms do bleed and feet do swell.
> Nail me down. Arms outstretched.
> Jaded ways. Someone I vexed.

Youthful dreams of gods and devils.
Demons forced screams
within this temple.

Abusing faith by coaxing hard length.
Beliefs, hearts,
full of loins and lions.

Wanting to get between my thighs?
Thinking correct placement?
Dark dungeon is the church basement...

    Spiritual debts to be broken!
    Collectors at the gates...
  May this be unspoken.

Never mind,
the function of subtle words.
Hidden meanings churn...

  In the grave.
  All words, stay the same.

{ The Valley of Negative Figures }

I stalk the valley of negative figures;
obscured by layers of painted muck.
Tainted eyes seeing only one truth.

Frigid hearts.
Unknown faces.

Stone walls calloused by bitter sands.
They walk slowly, carefully...
Unknown destination held by belief.

Heirs of the burden of motion;
placed forcibly in their minds.

Offspring of precision and authority.
Scalpel of a skilled surgeon.

Walk past pristine lakes.
Rivers encrusted,
entrusted with diamonds of sunlight.

Time to time seeing lost faces.
Face's outer covering.
Ripped flesh instead of filth.

Soul's forced.
Broken faces follow.

Their direction.
Their incision.
Their deviation.
Their indecision.
Their destruction.
Their infection.

Of negativity.
Of ignorance.
Of judgment.
Of truth.
Of anger.
Of bitterness.

Shining faces...

Foul herd!

Shoved and shat on.
Shoved and forced.
Nose in definite defecation.

Subjected to manipulative slicing.
They themselves had been subjugated,
too many years ago.

Radiant feces.

Tread lightly...
Pushed ever further by the crowd.
Tread lightly,
do not crush beauty.

Stifle a rose's journey...

Hearts are wicked...
Soiled soul.
Continued to trample.

Life ever marching.

No sight.
No reason.

Blind to such things.
Even logic.

Free mind lacking.
Never mind indoctrination!
Cell phone nation.

All taught toxins.
Barely seen faces...

!..among them..!

River in an ocean of sordid abyss.
Flow freely through this valley...

A place of rest.
A place of solace.
A place of embrace.

Negative souls raise up.
Dump waste and chemicals
into mind's eye.

Pollute the wonder of sight of beauty.
River. Poisoned...

Never clean again.
Dams cracked.
Impurities seep
into crystalline surface.

Never safe to swim.
Never safe drink from.

Emotional waters tainted.
Emotional banks eroded.

Negative figures...

Filling.
Overflowing.
Injected with toxins.

Polluted. Putrefied in hate.

Feces covered.
Plagued tongue. Sordid crowd.

Projecting their ways.
Negativity sold high.
Ashes of followers past.

I must escape this valley.

I must cleanse myself...

{ Reality's Curse }

Ever growing fears.
Basking in terror's glow.
Reinforcing what is already known.

Everything is gone.
Already dead.

Low tide faded memory.
Inside little heads.

A voyage to forgotten realm.
Childhood tales...
This wading pool we call life.

(Real or imagined?)

Eat the things that cum.
Digging in with violent strife.

What is gone?
Was it ever there?

Emptiness comes through.
Meditative stare?

The eyes of corpses.
Looking through you...

Would they call you by name?
If they only knew you?

Once had.
Forgotten tail.

Silence.

Now that it is gone...

Do you know you're unknowingly sad?
The beast still waiting to inhale.

Taken aback...
Bye living faded memory.

Sands of time,
all mean,
nothing.

How can you strive to survive?

Future so bleak.
When you know...

Reality's truth.
Reality's curse.

It is big and it is black,
it's called a hearse...

{ A Sleep's Close }

Form rests,
upon chair,
sleep takes hold.

Feeding on,
slice of existence,
desiccated and thrown away.

When eyelids flutter,
it all shall begin again,
brief parting from,
toils and troubles.

Bubble back,
forefront of mind,
ringing ensemble chimes in new day.

I shutter off to sleep.
Ending of beginnings weep.
Clutter of nocturnal abyss.

Sleeping eclipsed.

Perpetual rhythm of bleak turnstile,
to the River Styx.

Lay brain filled vessel down,
upon soft satin or cold stoic ground,
all the same.

Numbers counting down.
End this maze we walk.

Pennies please!

Counting down dates with X's.
Ferryman's toll...

Never notice small complexities.

Mutations spawning,
breaking time's unforgiving spindle.

Near to far seeing car to car,
purple woods and golden tar.

The tree's dance!
The moon is entranced.

Giggling gophers,
ramrod elegant peacocks.
Logic nor rules given black lace.
Rhyme before reason of shifted phase.

Have I returned?

What the Hell!

{ Mighty Cheese }

Blessed cow from whence cheese came,
Mother of Cheese.
Hollowed be Thy name.

Processor of Cheese, oh holy man.

To the packer of Cheese,
Holy Father, binder of cheese.
Thereby bringing about the
MIGHTY CHEESE unto us.

Unto the unworthy,
blessed carrier of the
Lord's mighty load.

To seller of Cheese whom Cheese
allows profits from
His Lordship.

Unto the eater,
Blasphemer of Mighty Cheese
and His Spirit.

For He who gave,
His only begotten
Single Severing Slice,
so we may all blaspheme,
and eat His brethren,
so bow down before Him
for without Him and His mighty
mother milk we would not
know the wonders we have today.

{ Silver Throat }

Bored, pondering,
how long this will take.

Water pulled and contorted.
Violent tornadoes,
down silver throat.

Rushing from the gash,
scurrying past these feet.
Yawn, watching fluid tendrils,
rush past me.

Body, past, flowing...
Drain to wonder.

Why was I created?
Worthless. Existence. Given.

Drain, watch it drain...
Out of steamy chamber.

Resting place.
Unforgiving dilemma spills forth.

Too hard.
Need, easy way out.
Cold crimson bath.

Peace...

{ Flaccid Decisions }

Splendor in pictures,
we don't want to see.

Finding roads to stumble on.
Nourishment sought. Hunger found.

Is the journey impotent?

Nourishes instincts,
flaccid decisions,
lost our standing.

Find giver gift.
Only to close eyes.

Walking forward.
Hitting the wall...

Will you fall?

{ Pissed Away Places }

Before last mile,
transversed unseen.

Pissed away places.
Unknown colors dreamed.

Today's gone by,
before what could have been.

Commit the first sin.
Thrust now good friend.

Lost youth.
Spent.

{ The Valley of Nocturnal Dreaming }

Into the valley,
of hallowed hills,
and bloodstained streets.

Holding to where roads do meet.
I look to stages of life;
only trying to be something someone.

Before.
I am.
gone...

Hold tight pillow.
Hoping monsters in shadows do lurk.

Monsters keep safe.
World normal travels.

Looking left, only heart beating.
Traveling valleys, alone.

Looking right, unknown darkness.
Time agonizingly passes.

Holding pillow tight,
fearful of the light.

Back to the road tomorrow...

{ Rocket Claimed }

Blast off! Rocket Fire Ln.
Life claimed.
Hands brought undue shame.
Force fed. Rocket claimed.

Take the fall...
Who's to blame?

Never live down.
Finger wrapped shame.

Whose name is on your lips?
Skin at your tips?

Do they still bring you tears?
Change you and bring new fears?
Words still ring in ears?

Just remember.

You gave them the power,
to destroy your cheers.

{ Drive the Need }

Filth on street,
came on the sheets,
blue gum on my shoe.

Lakes are polluted,
skies no longer blue.

Brown bark blackened,
by exhaustion.

Sordid world,
not worth coasting.

Made of chemicals,
no longer does it seed.

What good does this do?
What drives the need...

{ Top of the Pile }

Tumbling down a hole.
Dashed against rocks.
Again and again and again...

Endless bottom.

Will I reach origin again?
Trying to rise. Trying to rise.
What the fuck? I despise.
When you cannot even place,
one foot above the other.

Falling down.
Face down.
Withered acid pain.

Back to the opening pit.

Seeing light.
Crash down.
Again. Again. Again!

Will I ever stop falling?
Trying to break the fall.
No fall, at all.

How the hell can you stop...

Endless descent,
with no foothold to be found?

When you're not even close,
to the top of the pile.

Ace at the bottom,
never to rise to the top.

Never going to stop falling.

When you can't even stop...

Failing.

{ Holding Tight }

Walking sidewalk city,
sure sound of seen cries,
never before heard.

Eyes vomit waters blue,
seething waves,
ocean's fecal foam.

Seeping potent waves,
crushed against rocks,
meat holding tight.

Bleach waves,
crashing down corpse,
flopping breakers.

Night comes,
watch spirit's splash.

{ Cages for Sages ~ 4 }

Jars of stone,
jars of clay,
cages for sages,
will always say.

This not right.
This not wrong.

They dance.
They stutter.
They beat their dong.

Doves are for peace,
war is for man.

When everything is wrong,
is anything right?

When fear is,
the only true thing,
brought to light.

Midnight ticks closer.
Soon, I grow older.
Moments, pass away.
Spool of life shortens and...

{ Midnight Awaits }

Grave, one day will come.
X marks the new day.
Every day is just another way.
Goose step to end times.

Death's cold confines closer grow.
Heart beat cycle again,
futile cycle,
monotonous circle.

Tomorrow leads,
into stream of tomorrows.
Deadlights stare into midnight.
Nearer by the minute.
Come near me.

Into death we silently creep.

Life's joys should be enjoyed.
Drinks... drunk.
Friends: Smiles & Tears.

Midnight comes on those who wait.

Tomorrow will be just another date.

But wait...

Negate relativity to death's gate.
It's entrances it relates,
for tomorrow,
goodbye tonight.

Midnight!

Come closer to death's gate.

{ Date Rape Kisses }

Tomorrow leads screams.
Length grows longer.
Come near.

Fear, silently seeps.

Life enjoyed!
Drink. Drunk. Numb.

Friends... smiles became tears.
Danger, came at midnight.
Date rape kisses...

Want to live?
Don't tell the misses.

Entrance ripped kisses,
for tomorrow,
for tonight.

Hell's gate wishes...

Force wand,
closer to Devil's realm.

Sperm laden pressure cooker.
Left to boil over,
over, and over.

Trust...

Never.
The.
Same.

{ Adhesive Silhouettes }

Uniformity agitates these senses.
Erasing...

Complex. Unique. Rare.
Thoughts.

Suction adhesive silhouettes,
pasted on sheer mundaneness,
of suburban life.

Run past the draws of an easy life!
See the claws of what everyone,
wants everyone to be...

Like them!

Run!

But, pursuit is relentless.

Run. Run... Run!

But, sadly,
one day...

I will tire and fall shall I.

{ Skies of Pale }

Forced inside darkened room.
Shall this be my doom?

Holding tight memories' plume.
Smoke billowing senses.
Bewildered before moon's darkness.

Skies of pale.
Gray...

I wonder.

Of flame dwindling.
Of cold gush.
Of...

Never.
Being.
Young.

Will today be the last day?

Will it bring...
More pain than pleasure.

As always...

{ Forever Days }

Days may go by.
Winds may blow.
Nights will come.
On their way they go.

Hands on the clock,
make their way.

Around, ever-staring face...
But, that shall never change.

The love I have for you.

Years pass by.
Hours slip away.
Minutes go past.

But, this feeling shall never change.

Like, wind on my fingers.
Like, dust on my feet.

Forever days this heart does beat.
Depth, passion, flames.

Things always grow...

Old pictures fade.
Grass will turn brown.

Old. Age.

Root, dieting, dying in the ground.
Love, healthy, rooted deep in my soul.
No strong wind can pull.

I see your pulse.
Feeling your temperature rise.
Having never seen your eyes.

Golden soft heart.
Tempered glass...
Now, so soft.

Beat by its rhythm.
Pressure of the pulse.

Days will pass.
Love will prevail.

Over time.
Over age.

Because our hearts,
already passed the test.

{ Virtual Synthetic Suicide }

Why am I flying?
Below the waterline...
Drowning in good intentions.
Floating just above the surface.
Hearing cold waves vent force.
Shivering, shivering in silence.

Why are they crying out in the cold?
Tears becoming icicles.
Will the warm front come?
Frost on face.
Ice glass enclosed.

Why are the birds flying east?
Isn't that the road to death?

Frozen in flight...
Wings splitting.
Souls. Frigid and dying.

Flight of virtual synthetic suicide.
When did the world come to this?

Winter wonder psychosis land.
Still eyes lie and wait.
Opening spring gardens' gate.

A Heaven. A Hell.
Inside nice candy shall.

When the ice melts...
Do you cry or quiver?

{ Now Unfettered }

The nails of time,
draw down my back.

Sinew beneath bequeathed.
Flesh cracks.
Blood moves to stain.

Pulse slackens,
hair begins to mold,
age begins to creep,
moments silence deep.

Back bend commences,
time lets loose,
my secret of secrets,
lies now unfettered.

Will any of this matter?

Rusty cycle set in motion once more,
your transgressions betray you.

Is your sin a sin of a sin?

Can you... just be...
Fresh, new, and happy again?

{ Ever Unclean }

Want to see this pain in me?
Look, no further than the mirror.
Show your blankness.
Little bits of the past,
buried and forgotten.

A little twinge here.
Piece of paper memories.
Ripped plastic face,
that cries to no one.

Drive cars across me.
Wait! Have you lost me?
Just another crack in the soul.
Dust and dirt...

Ever unclean!

Wild abandon of the ever unseen...
Last thing you'll see.

Bitter ice of winter's bite...
Mirror's fog,
cold summer's night.

Our own cries...
Blowing dust.
Blinded by sun's varying light.

Ever knowing reflections
of tired lines.

Small spots showing
all the cracks we hide.

But. Thankfully...

Too many flaws,
to be able to decipher or decide.

{ Fear of the Bright }

Spikes of sunlight darkness.
Hinges, frame's forgotten creak.
Open pain fades as
guarded towers crumble.

Making fear arise.

This time.
No malice.
Comes forth.

Expressing yourself, so hard...
Eyes opening beyond boundaries.
Conscious mind. Held back?

A kindled brilliance radiates,
fills the sober corners of your mind.
Flashlight peers through,
obscure cave tonight.

Time to escort you,
through this cavern.

To see past all the dismay,
and the fear of the bright.

{ Rose Colored Destruction }

Breath of the Gypsy,
whipping through buildings,
sending papers to nowhere.
Traveling every nook, dilapidated.
Until it flaps
browned timeworn curtains.

Blood of the Gypsy,
flowing gutted waters.
Carving a path.
Splashing to and fro
without clear purpose.

Never journey's ending will come.
No respite from wearying path.

Kiss of the Gypsy,
still on lips.
Haunting dreams...
Just beyond fingertips.
Aching for the scent of a feeling,
once again...

Life of the Gypsy,
never held too tightly.
Forward forever looking.
Never forgetting who's left behind,
in rose colored destruction.

Death of the Gypsy,
in unknown spaces.
Last thoughts of a million places.
Skin, bone, and faces.
Left behind.

{ Dirt Petals }

I smell the shit,
upon the tongues of power.

I inhale shit,
from the begging of urchins.

Dung muddled voices.

Words seeping lies,
made of feces and rot.

Holding onto old ways.
Always admiring...

Someone.
Else's.
Shit.

It's a world of dough.
It's a world of wit.
It's a world of lies.
It's a world of shit.

Crap contaminates life,
love is sorrow.

Feces of clown's joy,
dirt petals.

Knelling in it,
bowing face first...

Just praying shit gets better...

LIES!

{ Dream Web }

Can of ground confusion,
poured into,
seeping vats of vomit.

Whatever became of the tailor?

Will you weave,
colorful dream web,
of gilded entrails?

Brain: rotted-smelling cantaloupe.
Nothing more.

Unrelenting spasms,
frigid cruel broken down crèmes,
that left a stain.

Apply carefully to head & shoulders.

Where blood has been erased.
It suddenly occurs to me!

Only disgrace is success.

Defile the flesh I inhabit!
Please...

{ Whispers of Death }

Silken skin softly,
offers smooth caress.

Too many days have passed,
since before.

Alas, too few times show,
what is soul.

Glistening dreams,
past what may come again.

No surety,
knowing these things.

Only finality in death,
until then...

Enjoy.
Every.
Breath.

{ Dear Girl }

Take a bite of my apple...
Dear girl.
Taste the sweet juices.

Take a look inside yourself...
Dear girl.
See the treats that I offer.

Take my caress...
Dear girl.
Feel yourself melt away.

Take a trip into my eyes...
Dear girl.
Find yourself.

Take your time...
Dear girl.

Take yourself...
Dear girl.

I know that beyond those eyes...
There is a beating heart.

Take my apple...
Dear girl.
Enjoy the sin of my sweet juices.

{The Taste of Purple is Made of Cheese}

The night is blue; the day is gray.
Holding onto darker days.

Once again with the bloody ham!

Diamonds are for the fire?
Wind runs higher...
Hard flows the stones like water.

No more mirrors.
No more fears.

Dead is the twine,
of the midnight cherry.

Night forgot spark,
for the snow.

The ash breaks the iron;
cold stone pudding.

Singing to the gasses,
of broken bone glasses.

{ A Valley of Laughter }

I walk to a valley of laughter.
Seeing the shine of a dime.
Seeking worlds of light and darkness.
Bound together in time.
World of light, world of darkness.
Frightening, only for a moment.
Spark lightning sun bathing.
My eyes burning with easy lies.
Holding my tongue neglected.
Grasping bloody heart.
Shouldn't have waited.

Passion torching flash...

Not mine!

Looked, listened,
and waited: endless time.

Crushed and downtrodden...
No care from hearts and minds,
I once shared.
From then until now as dark unto light.
I am a shining dark fright.
Fight in obscure night.
Looking forward to journeys unknown.
Who knows whom will care,
what my heart will had known.
With spirit and rhyme,
darkest of night.

One and soon many be by my side...

So, now...

Let us travel to valleys unknown.

{ Glass Smiles }

Glass Smiles,
all that graced the face...

Ever shattered on the floor,
hearts thinking, maybe.

Did not think,
too scared to think...

Dreads to think,
those are not glass smiles anymore.

Looking into fiery eyes of tomorrow.
Will possibilities become realities?

The heart knows?
Lips listen to formed smile.
Real?

Vicious vivacious smile...
Not known for quite a while.

It makes hearts wonder.
Fears arise!
Behind that smile.
Behind those eyes.

Call calm fears.
They calm.
They calm.
Please... calm...

Quell them and fly away.
Whizzed, wasted, washed...

Smile widens...
Continue to do so?
See inside fears?
Brushed away...

Smile true?
Heart? Mind? Face?
No more cracked smiles...
Anymore.

{ Pushing to Enjoy }

Skin slowly creeps.
Slinking out of the flesh.
Too attack its enemies!
Force fed enemas.
Shield it from outside forces.

Pushing to enjoy,
the fruits of its labors.

Striking out by breathing.
The skin it follows suit.

Withered by age.
The first to give up.
Leaving, its job is done.

{ The Sun }

A luminous day is upon us.
A heart and this misery.
The heat from children of the night.

A shower of light...
She brings.

It taints our happy places.
Walking past, seemingly dead.

Nothing different.

Stone walls. Stone walled.
Silver night makes them thrive.

Vibrant.
Vivacious.
Voracious.

Alas, this day is broken.
It breaks down our contentment.

Makes it hot.
Makes it shine.

It hurts these eyes.
Scorches fragile retinas.

Wait until nocturne.
Bids us draw near.

Once.
More.

{ Nightmares Grown Old }

For every spark of light,
inside there is darkness.
A bright star black hole.
Angel-eyed poet. Wild-eyed madman.

Heart of a demon.
Soul of an angel.

Disguised by black of night.
Hidden in broad daylight.
Holding on to happiness tight.

Holding anguish, rage, and hate...
Not far from sight.
Hidden, hiding, horror!

Scared of bright days,
and darkest nights.

I see hate in happiness,
soothing my soul.

They both delight me cold.
Nightmares grown old.
Time to be told, shine bold.

Old, cold, alone...
I'm home.

{ Only Demons Can Fly }

Tar clouds overcoming the dawn.
World clangs in anticipation.
Mist in the wind.

Morning fear mourning.
Ascending from the nether regions.

Pain that will sear.
Scar that shall itch.
A mouth shall be stitched.

Rigid grate,
an order to assimilate.

A hand will rise against,
cynical demise.

Slime black mold
charcoal cold,
blood spills,
for those who hold...

A light to the sky,
as now only demons can fly.

{ Nights of Autumn and Early June }

Look away,
from patronizing day

Wait for pain,
hoping to find remains.

Holding passion's dream.
Reliving night's caresses.

Waking before dawn,
standing in dewlight.

Looking for solace and comfort in dusk.
Because, days are broken.
Nights are scattered, shattered,
memories worn, torn, and tattered.

Hold on to the breath.
Gentle sway, rock & roll wind.

Night or Day?

Night eyes supple wrap.
No longer in human skin dressed.

Smile and look to the blood moon,
think of Autumn and early June.

Where days were long and I was alive.
Meandering in this dank dark dive.

Forgiven memories of when I died...

{ Uncaring Passion }

Here's the gray plague of indifference.
An uncaring passion
dies in complacency.

Dazzling, nimble creatures,
bounding without hindrance.

This poison takes hold too rapidly!
Slowly, we are all infected.

Joys are contaminated.
Degenerated.

Smiles become betraying tears shown.
Both living/dead.

Hearts and minds,
grayed like ashes.

Passions have disengaged,
disintegrated,
incinerated.

What is it that will
surpass this toxin,
that invades fragile pathways?

No cure came till almost all died.
Still one left in tragic fields.

Flights of grave indifference.
Short sanctuary.
A hope of beauty's perseverance.

Time's wick turns to black;
time is nearly done,
poison cannot be outrun nor contained.

As it is in all things;
in all places,
in all forms,
taking root in the gravel.

Smothering all emanations of emotion.
Nothing heals!

One pulse still runs...

Still waits...
for beauty's return

{ Beauty in Cruelty }

The beast walks blood stained sheets,
looking for a meal,
writhing from the hunger,
an urge for meat.

Pain migrates to all touched.
Lusting for before times,
before all was blood and gore.

Loosely holding tampon strings.
Life's bloody bullshit.

Straining to...

Fight.
The.
Urge.

Compromising my nature.
Beauty in cruelty.

Wait in the alley.
Wait for the day.

I will... take your breath away...

{ Feeling the Drain }

Darkness and devils,
fire and lice,
pests and vermin,
roaches and mice.

They bite at your feet,
like rats at the dead,
eating away at the brain in your head.

Making you weak, feeling the drain.
Drug fire light making you insane.

{ The Valley of Corpses }

I walk the valley of corpses.

Trying to find unknown faces.

Always seeing further than always seen.

Habit wins. Habit descends.

Drives forward obscene.

Want. Need. Desire.

Running past the peak.

{ Children of the Nails }

Following like children at the zoo.
Wondering if the sun will rise again.

Son now fallen!
Fallen by choice.

Cool wind chilling.
Frigid hearts.
Warmed by his death.

Unconcerned.
Because: lies.

Cold and dead.
Only human.

Not a single tear shed.
When the son fell.

Night reclines,
hearing their call.

Zombies never walked,
among the living...

Darkness is...

One moment,
another dead brain cell.

Because another preacher,
came too quickly on their masses.

Arctic whites,
charcoal blacks,
zombie grays.

Coffin fairy tales.

Do not lend them aid.
Do not give them,
benefit of a diagnosis.

They. Need. Lies.
Death to the light!

Keep them productive.
Keep them quiet.
Keep them stupid.

Children of the nails.

{ The Heart }

Rubbing away the rough edges.
Pieces were askew.

Fresh paint carefully, slowly,
applied to soft heart.

Protect it with thick coating,
so words cannot hurt.

Allowing beauty to realize radiance.

{ Wedding Bows }

Spheres roll down flesh.
Ducts are spent.
Nothing left.
Heart purged.

Weaved words so inept.
Knowing wretched distance flown.
Taking my uniqueness,
making existence,
an unworthy experience.

Measure the gain,
bitterness considering worth.

Giving and receiving a fecal charade.

Why is death the only reason,
people grieve on this earth?

Sullen faces in happy parades,
leaving futile cardboard cases.

Placing...

Carefully,
artfully,
finishing touches,
on their mausoleum.

Betrayed by bride and groom's,
soon-cracked faces.

Superstitions and morticians.
Mutual infinite wisdom?
Fools!

Without priestly precision.
Vows said: broken, done.
Quick steady movements.
Said, spread, and done.

How can I be potent?
When everything is impotent.

Do not forget on the spreading day...

This is nothing more than...

A man's arrogance.

and

The games women play.

{ Future's End }

A room,
a view,
something askew: it's missing you.

Where did everything go?

Days of old.
Sublime untold.

You where there.
Life grew old.

Cold, but wait,
new blood creeps free.

Behold! New person quiver.

Voice shiver night.
Shadows fright light.

Wait, what is this sight?
You stand there in fright.

How cold are you now?

Someone crying...
Something staining...

Standing above you.

You said.
You saw.

The future in me.

You.
Were.
Right.

Future's end.

{ Our Moaning }

Gusts breathed through my hair,
gentle breeze,
threw me upon the ground.

Try to hold force,
albeit a firm caress prevailed.

Struck like stones.
Hands grew weak.
Heart grew old.

Grasped what once was.
Hoped to maintain this stance.
Knowing all is lost.

All our memories...
Mammaries.

Our dreams.
Our moaning.

Made us numb.
Rendered us vulnerable.
No mercy.

Save that opportunity to surrender.

To their whims.
Held on to time,
wanted to escape.

Impossible pursuit.
Recaptured...

Hold on to all moments!

That subtle smile.
A nimble touch.

Because when all is gone...

Nothing remains.
But memory...

{ Drug of Choice }

Crash and burn;
rise from cinders of death.

Ashes of the never would could.

Broken and free.

The strongest fall to their knees,
for their master.

Who is the drug of choice.

{ Sips from Turpentine }

The glass is full.
Clear liquid bids me draw close.
The smell corrodes the air.

Making nostrils burn,
eyes water, the scent becomes,
increasingly tantalizing.

A wish the day had gone better.
A wish life had substance.
A wish I could fulfill something.
A wish everything
in this letter mattered.
A wish my words were as strong,
as this vapor now enveloping me.

Destabilizing embrace,
warmer still than that of those...

Whose memory scarcely lingers.
Whose hearts emerged unscathed.
Whose minds asked few questions.

Their tears will flow freely.
Their moans will be heard
from a distance.
Their screams shall break glass.

Pain will bore them.
Memories shall fade
from time's sterile hand,
with great surgical skill.
Time infects bodies with tumors.

My deepest affection to all.
Heart not jaded.
Set free from this curse.

This sickness is not me.

The earth shall not hesitate
upon its poles.
Nor the moon fall behind
in drawing tides.

Desire a slave?
Search one out.

I will not be found on my knees,
marring myself with groveling pleas.

So I sit here in darkness.
No companions save this soliloquy,
and this glass of caustic spirits.

To think, they thought me,
irrational enough,
to do such a thing in haste!

Enjoying the fragile smoothness
of this glass.

Begin benign slumber.
Filling my mind.
Making uncertain moments pass.

Altered for better.
Course of one little life.
Garnered no virtue.
So enjoy my isolated altruism.

My fate.
My trap.
My point of origin.

Returning?

Join me in paradise city.

Where sips of turpentine can be,
for one or for three.

{ Lost & Found }

All is not lost.
You can still be found.
If you only look to your heart.
Not to the ground.

{ Golden }

Looking at tomorrow.
Thinking cf yesterday.
Watching lights in my head blink...

On, off, on, off.
Sitting and looking
at yesterday's tomorrows.

I wonder.
I ache.
I tremble.

I sit looking at today's tomorrows.

What became of the dreams dreamed...

I felt I was at...
my summit of achievement,
at the pinnacle of this life.

Set the spires ablaze.
Watched towers crumble.

Can you keep stoking the fires?

Hopes self-destructed. Nobody is here.

Sit and watch tomorrows run.

From life.
From death.

Wanting both!
Nothing left...

I sit and wait thinking of tomorrow.
Wanting it to be different!
...than yesterday...

Some way...
Anyway.
Every way...

I sit...
Wanting; hoping...
Grinding/groping.

Bits of sanity...
Madness sets me free.

But for what?
To be me?
How can I be free to be me?

I'm locked away where no one can see...
Holding onto hope.
Am I foolish?

Groping for insanity...

Set me free from this cage.
Insidious rage.

One grave.
Living grave.
Grave details.

Waving at the seashells,
holding purple flags,
flying golden flags.

Insistent, twice curved corner clown,
smiling into the eyes,
of a dead child.

One fierce day...

Everyone goes away,
having too much to say.

Nothing is said today.

One golden child...

Too many miles.
Blinking lights do defile.
Eve of deadly deed does not end...

How do I let go?

Insanity and I

Too often have a drink together.

Blinking lights keep flashing,
Pinwheel spins all the while,
defiled little smile frowns,
trying to get away.

One thing.

"One thing... I will say."

(It is never just one thing.)

Saying the thing in spring!
A spring in your step before you wept.

Dated old chair,
is it time slept?

Greatest burden of beasts,
with eyes burnt.

Haven't you heard them?
Can't you hear them?

Wasting a day...
Wasting away.
Golden days. Golden ways.

Lost in a day's daze haze.

Hopeless hearts,
weeping silent tears,
rolling crushing defeat.

All we do is get old.
Lost spring whispers.

Dandelion dew.
Bone.
Blood chilled through.

Do you want something?
What do you want?
How much?

There is no nonsense.
Is this nonsense?

Do you want to live!
Making hearts ache.

We struggle to keep our mouths above,
indefinite mud.

Careless jitters
from inordinate whispers.

Simple wands moving around inside,
as a crown and a frown.

Is that painting upside down?

Where do you flow?
To whom do you go?

Have you all forgotten all?

Will this time,
be forgotten.

Last caress of death,
find peace,
in your first breath.

Breathe in and out until you are deaf.

One more thing before I go!
Will I go?

You... Do. Not. Know.

For me,
life is all a show,
for my amusement and your abusement.

Beat your mind,
rape your soul,
so you choose it.

Breaking me won't be easy.
No it won't be done.

...I'm already broken...

Do not think you're the only one.
Go inside dying bride.

Simple neck caresses.

Now, nothing left.

Golden anvil of life,
meets silver mallet of death.

Waiting and wanting for final breath.

Golden.

{ Black Blood Stains }

I am drowning in a sea of sorrow.

Days,
breaking...

Earth,
quaking...

Life,
shaking...

Each day,
every day...

    We breathe.

Step inside and see!

Negativity,
fester.

Pain,
sequestered.

    Within.

You feel.
You think.
You know.

Black blood stains,
all just the same.

Dead heart beats.

Beneath,
flesh sheet.

One more person,
to meet.

Before the days,
go away.

The sun shined today?

Passion meets peril,
thankfully sterile.

There's never a death,
like that of the breath,
that forms when someone,
speaks the words...

　　　I love you.

{ Zip My Pants }

Taking you hard and fast,
getting what I want.

Pushing your head in the water,
getting a thrill,
knowing I may not be your first,
but forever will I be your last...

Pulling behind you,
lust fills my eyes with burning hatred.
I pull
glimmering metal blade from its sheath.

Coming soon to your skin.

Delicate red streaks.
Your arms go limp.

It's exciting me all the more.
I'm over the top!

Shooting into limp carcass.
Gazing upon rust streaks,
Wetting your hair more.

Warmth drained.
Limp vessel.

Feeling cold breath on my neck.
Suddenly, I realize what I've done.

Are you standing there?
Frozen in the moment.

I zip my pants quickly.

Turning.
Running.

Quickly out the door I escape.

Unknowing of my fate,
for deeds done.

{ Red Satin Caress }

Short moments spent together,
lingering in my mind.

Permanently affixed to my being.

The tears.
The ecstatic smiles.

Your fear.

Warm moments of silence.
Ring fresh in my ears.

In my eyes,
sounds of your strained voice.

Echoes across mental terrain.

The scent of your hair.
Lingers on my sheets.

Dreams of repeat performance.

Soft, red, satin caresses,
blanketing my flesh.

Reverberating through this soul.

What was lost.
Again shall be.

A look of the eyes.
Flesh meeting flesh.

I invite you to...

Spend eternity in my soul.
Letting linear things crumble.

I will drink you in.

So, you'll...

Never be far from me.

{ The Moon }

Hands of a ghost upon my face.

Seen never eyes.
Makes blood race.

Breath frozen walk.
Whispers on my skin.

Think of that day.

Ghost. Silk. Flesh.

Flash of hands,
on my throat.

Still I can discern dead eyes.
Though, physical form, rotted long ago.

She hopes to see fear's reflection.
Reflected in my eyes.

Tortures not temporal or ethereal.
Soon shall be my fate...

I do not repent!

{ Devils Fear the Dead }

Golden moments deceased.
By this beast inside my head.
Now, devils fear the dead.

Previous little deaths,
laid upon my bed.

The baseline came to my line,
in headlines of my mind.

Ever-flowing never-knowing,
façade cracking,
fear ever showing.

Heatwave in my grave,
it's time I'm given,
graven images that I gave.

A heart released by the knife,
every sin, now,
bursting into the light.

Slipping away,
falling away,
into darkening day.

This is the time.
The time.
I pay.

Grasping at straws.
Drinking from life.

Zeroing in on the end,
of my razor knife.

Fight. Flight. Fatigue.

Weeping follows.
Whimpers and swallows.

Gripping my fingers,
at the lost fragments,
of my forgotten tomorrows.

With a brain full of lead.

I must say,
goodnight...

{ The Valley of Fear }

We walk the valley of fear.
Seeing seething pits of despair;
falling into traps
of misery and loneliness.

A valley very different.
Loneliness real not imagined.

Faces of the past,
only dreams and spectacles,
that once filled life.

Only fading memories,
remain.

In the valley of fear.

Surviving, intense struggles,
against lines,
drawn in the sand.

Bye shadow figures...

Sun has gone,
shadow figures dissipate,
into bleak tomorrows.

Life once filled with joys,
I could not enjoy.

Hindered by,
lack of understanding,
of what happiness actually was.

Now, only now,
comprehending,
lost possibilities.

All. Done. Now.

Hope for the chance,
to once again live happy...

To leave this valley,
to escape these sorrows,
we must move on...

Before it envelopes all.

{ Blown Flatulence }

Incongruities of,
this immature world.

Soft spoken fan,
of outspoken babble,
in which we dabble.

Look out for the faithful!
All too much escapism...

Embittered ways,
reminding daily,
of mediocre solace...

Antiquated youthful dreams.
Stray adolescent screams.

Watch mercury lowered,
broken God.

See frigid maids gathered,
bores for the taking.

Ring comes to finger,
end of dreams.

Blown flatulence,
childhood tales fail miserably.

As heart beats and face pales.

Gusts will subside,
no more trying.

Crust begins to form,
as the joys of ceremony,
are so quickly...

Just a memory.

{ Negativity of Demons }

Standing in the light,
negativity of demons...

Beckons me.

A life,
once held,
once glorious,
now broken,
melted.

Grasping dark failures,
calling them brilliance,
warm night blanket,
cushioning my fall.

No negativity.

But, how hard,
will the ground be,
after I jump?

No demon blanket,
laid out,
to nestle in.

Pulling back,
negativity repressed...

I want to live!

Gravity oppressed...

Will my soul find peace?
Due to earth's caress.

Ending in pain just as it began.

With negativity's laugh...

It was too late.

{ Numbing Touch }

Hold on golden fire.
Smear the cream of rigid angels.
Maintaining gelatinous form.

Consecrate them,
abstractly,
in mind's eyes.

A face eternally malleable.

Mold sets in,
rhyme rhythm renders hearts,
riddled with holes.

Carelessly gored by your...

Uncaring words,
violent penetration,
numbing touch.

Closing my eyes,
just to forget I'm here.

{ Pins & Needles }

She's made of,
pins and needles.

She spends her leisure with,
black-backed beetles.

Her glittering exterior,
is but a façade,
for ash-black interior.

Caught up desperately,
in the webs of existence.

She hears white noise,
off in the distance.

Obscurity calls,
her inner being.

Nights alive with writhing.
Too far above inner clearing.

There is...

Forgiveness.
Ecstasy.
Awakening.
Relapse.

Waiting in lines for broken dreams.

With trembling hands,
stitching anew their fragile seams.

How do we know,
when it is time to depart?

When the infinite abyss,
engulfs our hearts.

{ The Night }

Clouds glow serenely,
in the dark sky night.

Moon ablaze,
flecks of glitter and haze.

Starlight flows,
in my eyes,
like waves upon an ocean,
of darkness and dreams.

Embracing feelings,
of warmth flowing from fingertips.

Displays of splendor,
that are the night.

Shadows enveloping me,
in sweet abyss.

My eyes burning daylight,
into eyes entrenched...
and shadows of evils,
the true obscenity,
that is humanity.

For now, feed me,
mental syrup.

Lie to me.

Let peace,
feel real.

{ Limbo or Lobotomy }

Walking into another's thoughts.
Consoled despair was for naught.

In a moment,
bitter fires grew dim.

Within soon extinguished.
Time's lapsed words,
fashioned of glass...

Now...

Only slipping, sliding,
shattering from,
uncomfortable glances.

Desolation of former times,
still lies within.

But...

Now, I!

Saint becomes sinner.
I cannot pray for forgiveness.

Do not feel deserving of penance.

Only purgatory.
Limbo or lobotomy.

Experiences give insight anew.

Contributing ever-changing points view.
Knocking all our mirrors askew.

I have failed myself.

I failed you.

Helpless to alter this path formed.

We will never again...
Feel our presences!

No embraced.
No warmed.

Simply memories of warmer days.

{ Rain }

Rain. Gaze. Sky.

Drops falling,
trickling down,
rolling down,
my cheek.

Pondering rain's,
indifferent droplets,
walking in the rain,
roll down these arms,
hiding these tears.

Want. Given. Release.

Blood through veins.

Exit Strategy.

Feeling numb, cold.

Slowly splitting,
drenched deluge,
fantastic hues,
no subtle cues.

I'm tired...

Final rest for the weary.

{ All Beautiful Things }

All see the world.

Wonderful place of lies.

Unicorns shitting,
cotton candy and rainbows.

Blame God Everything.
Unable to control.

Hate to start,
letting excuses,
into our souls.

Seeping and tainting,
all beautiful things.

{ The Weapon Curse }

We look.
We question.
Everything.

Giving rise to our,
depressive minds.

We depress life's buttons,
to find answers,
too many answers.

Always wondering,
if you're right or wrong.

Hope is dead,
in the eyes,
of the drained.

Eyes of the starving,
strive for logic,
but find no peace...

Looking for happiness... deceased.
Our roots,
withered and decaying.

Hoping this hole inside,
is bled dry.

Six inch valley,
inside my skull.

Deep scalpel swimming,
in deep red floods,
deep in the sand...

Time's tool,
the weapon curse.

Just one day,
to ride in a hearse.

So try hard,
to remember.

We're not dead...

Yet.

It is not time,
to let go...

So, please,
enjoy this moment,
with me.

Enjoy all things,
but don't think,
too much.

You might break your springs.

{ Night's Past Beginning }

An awakening...

Looking,
for food,
for solace,
for comfort.

Awaken as the sun,
falls to slumber;
gazing to the east...

Seeing hardened eyes,
of night's past beginning.

Arising, finding...

Nothing.

{ Fuck Enlightened Futures }

In a world of chaos and sweat,
times shall come to vent,
sweet frustrations.

Finales we will see,
a lifetime's,
failure prosperity.

Rise above the phoenix!
Shoot past ashes, soot, and flames.

Burst forth,
in cold euphoric fury;
freezing stop flight,
wings destroyed shattered.

Fuck enlightened futures!

Make phoenix crash,
unrepentant frost gash,
replenish the land.

Investing inviting shadows,
shunning truth and understanding.

Negate closed open-mindedness!

Who wants reality?

Not those for the sake of comfort,
who would dare attempt to quell,
understanding.

Violent ends in fiery wake.
Common enough.

Uncommon frigid gaze,
beyond correctness haze.

Shall one?
Look to carrion eyes.

Your bird of fire,
will be silenced,
by souls of ice.

{ River of Reversal }

Rationality lost control.
Seeping through the sieve.
Looking through life.

It ages.
It swims.
It slithers.

I drown.

In one uniform breath.

I see you.

In this river of reversal.

I want you...

...to die.

{ Feast of Joy }

Sky fire drains.
Bitterness from the heart.

All you've done.
All of your hate.

Opened these dreaded gates,
wounds set winter free.

This beast finds prey,
lashes out.

Please, cry into the night.

So I can...

Chuckle at your pain.

I feel...

Your sadness.
Your bitterness.
Your anguish.

Feast of joy...

I relish a hearty laugh,
at all of your tears...

Your crime is greater.

The very leader of hell,
does not deserve.

The vile treachery,
for which you now pay in full.

You are dead inside.
Dead. To. Me.

Your coal,
black as night,
burns my fire,
lights my desire to destroy.

No diamond could you be.

Do you truly believe,
you deserve happiness?

After ripping skin from bones,
heart from soul.

You are miserable, wretched fools;
always trying to swim upstream.

You're worthless salmon!

Die, you fucks!

Die, so those who deserve,
what you had,
may come and take your place.

Eat yourself and die! As your kind do.
Destroy everything you love...

Start again.

The coals turn gray,
as shattered trinkets are wont to do.

All memories fade,
only souvenirs remain,
to remind of your sordid smiles.

Claims laid calm.

Holding onto your wasted games.
Waiting for your day of shame,
to befall you.

So bitterness can no longer,
be happiness.

{ I Burn Sprouts }

I am the beast,
the world of inside-out,
spittoons up-your-downs.

I burn sprouts and I burn around,
I take fire you feed upon light.

I am scared of the day and the night.
Too many springs make too many falls.

What are we supposed to do?

Care about it all...

{ The Tear }

Dry those eyes,
you've found the end to lies.

Truth...

In the ear.
In the eyes.

One day then two passes bye.

Holding on, hypnotize.

No falsehood;
cremated dreams, begin to rise.

Slashing movements,
shall drift away.

Tearing away,
anguishes of yesterdays.

Truth came in totality forms.

I loved,
my sweet death.

Breathing again. Thought to be nigh.
Heart beating once again.

These lips,
have not given,
their last sigh.

Wait a minute!
Truth is here.
Have no fear!

Integrity has replaced the tear.

{ Queen Never }

Eyes, glowing at night.

Might shrinks,
from heat of her light.

Once great king falls,
from choice of mate.

She now rules,
untimely fate.

Flowing freely,
wind whispers darkly,
across her warm smile of ice.

Clouding his judgment,
of ones,
once thought wise.

What of all the poisons,
which fill his mind?

Will he ever see the blindfold,
laid on his eyes?

No!
Thank you...
Queen Never.

Sadly, his end is near.
Happily, so is her demise.

Townsfolk see...

Her treachery.
His pains.

Seizing the day,
As their beloved king,
fades away.

This shall be the day,
they,
tore her limbs away.

{ The Valley of Concrete }

They walk in the valley of concrete,
Longing for days...
Days of soft greens and piercing blues.

Gazing at towers of glass,
and hearts grown cold.

Bodies ache for things of the past.
Minds glowing with future plans.

And for what...

Progress you say?

Progress, disassembling purity,
in an angular world.
Is progress green skies and
hay-colored grass?

Is progress understanding everything?

For the sake of nothing.

Walking,
cracked paved roads,
now lined by empty concrete husks,
cluttered with a trillion empty dream.

Once was this a field?

The foliage has died,
beneath the rejectamenta of humanity.

They walk through,
the valley of concrete,
where they see,
the shadows of the past...

A crystal blue sky,
jade grass,
shimmering drinkable waters.

They wonder,
once,
shadowed by concrete...

Will it even matter?

Moving on...

{ Eye Windows }

Hands char my skin.
Desires fuse to this flesh.
Reality's finite possibilities.
Render those heated moments eternal.

Until then,
handle time with care.
Disregard mortality's stare.

Heart aches for touch.
Soul begs for eye windows.

Nostrils yearn,
for the smell of your skin.

Fingers need sensation of hair.

Will you soon dwell in my heart,
or shall we
both grow old and die apart?

{ Fallen Abyss }

Hearts abused and battered.
Taken for granted,
by fools who shattered.

Beauty.

More foolish still,
those who thought there was,
no heart.

When the core was a cavity,
broken apart.

Oh, how ignorance makes,
such a faulty hypothesis.

When treated with an emptiness;
fallen abyss.

Blood still,
makes its winding course,
through otherwise broken body.

Each touch,
brings reverberation.

Do not disclose this.
They could be one of them.

Toying with your soul,
for novel amusement.

Breaking your strings.
Dislodging your joints.
Weathering your smile.

Hiding is better,
than letting them,
kill all that you are.

{ Black Roses }

Darkened eyes silent.
Quickly cast down.
Muted screams echo.
Shaded shattered grins.

Rotten bodies writhing.

The sounds of liquid shit torrents,
reverberate through these halls.

Blood reigns,
where the black roses grow.

Thorns pricking your fingers,
making numb.

Tears run down,
making dumb.

Emotions,
fertilize well.

How can this heart feel,
loathsome inner Hell?

With...

No day.
No knight.
No armor.
No fight.

Just enough time for,
fairy tale fantasy execution.

{ Fiendish Flesh }

Eyes look down,
beckoning to follow,
after the night,
daybreak moonlight.

Day destroyed by,
nights bloom's fall.

Filling eyes,
with fever hunger.

Lust flowing freely,
night quakes to be released.

Walking daylight.
Waking preylight.

Dazed as hunger breeds,
walking through scents,
that surround me.

Tasting,
lust in the air.

The scent of one's hair,
brushes of fiendish flesh.

Shivers...

Run.
Down.
Spine.

Hunger overcomes reason.

Lust breaks free...

To chase.
To claw.
To bite.
To ravage.

All sensibility, lost.
The day has come!

Now...
Fun!

{ Bottom of Being }

Pain;
it builds,
it beckons...

Torture,
it weeps into veins,
it fills the soul,
numbness comes to fruition.

Holding these emotions at bay.
Scraping the bottom of being.

Only fragments,
of former agonies remain.
Silent in torment.
Words running together.

This empty existence.
This worthless life.

Their tattered remains.
These lost little emotions.
Only a tired weakened corpse here.

Rendered shale,
by their hands.

Those same hands groped,
at my intestines.

The hands that grasped,
at the blood,
as it flowed through my veins.

Needles behind my eyes.
Hands, do not belong,
moving lower, mutilating me.

Growing accustomed,
to the sting.

Eventually,
beautifully,
numb.

Torture to breathe.

Soul of trash,
longing for,
the soft caress of death.

A cold touch,
never allowing,
that final solution.

Always...

Always keeping me,
dead alive...

Striving for a moment of solace.

Knowing it will never come.
One can only be...

The lady of sorrow.
The lady of chaos.

Those eyes entrapped,
the sweet numb death.

That needle prick,
still comes in,
from time to time.

No conflict.

Her demise.
Her ending.
Her silence.
His joy.

All suffering is beauty;
so broken.

{ On My Plate }

At the dinner,
of silent bitterness.

You are the disease,
on my plate.

Heated meatballs,
float in gelatinous gravy.

Your flesh a gift,
on my table.

Giving thanks to,
these misgivings collected.

The poisons: filter on life's plate.

My listless palate emaciates me.

Your moistened flesh,
is my sickness.

No scars shall form,
on the meal that is you.

{ Your Happiness }

Tracing your pain.

Locating the entrance,
to your scars.

Ripping this burdensome nettle,
from your eye.

Drain the pains,
from your veins
only memories remain.

Hold hands,
pulling through,
spike-laden spirit pit.

Mind unraveling.

This. Is. What I do.

I am control.

Grasping, tightly.
Making certain to rip lives.

I, the needle in your veins.

Injected,
I need your pains.

Do not push away.

I do NOT approve.

Of your happiness,
without my permission.

{ The Sorrows of Skin }

Walking to the edge of tomorrow.
Looking to forever yesterday.
Seeing a place inside life.
Where all is nothingness.

Never exist in tomorrow,
last Wednesday.

Falling to pieces,
the sorrows of skin.

Calloused.
Crumbled.
Cried.

Take little comfort,
in places of silence.

Run! Must run!

Hear the thunder of heavy machinery.

In. My. Head.

A heart heavy,
silenced by clamor and commotion.

Growing older is inevitable.
Growing up should be challenged.

At. Every. Step.

I walk through the valleys.
I look to the summits.

I wonder.

Why do they tell me to follow the herd?

Moo.
Moo.

No!

{ Nightmare Fantasy }

I, your dreams,
a nightmare fantasy.

I, the thing,
that makes you bleed.

Trapped in nightmare,
of the so called happy world.

Hand cuffed to lies,
of Heaven and of Hell.

Sin in the cathedral,
of swine.

Wooden goblet. Carpenters cross.

Burning the wood,
tossed in the line of fire survival.

Thin bolts of white fabric,
frocked in stained sheets.

Forgiven of misgivings,
wave bye now...

Just words: I am forgiven!

Ribbon of purple, ribbons of gold...

Restless merriment,
subdued by frantic whiners.

No more bowing,
because to you,
everyone is a sinner.

{ Demons Cry Sleeping }

Fragments of my soul,
gone forth without me.

Crucial parts,
of existence gone.

Holding memories void,
grinds my heart.

Pestle to mortar,
scratching this bitch.

Form changes,
but integrity, never.

The already reunion,
by so close separation.

Dreaming and maintaining,
obscuring and losing.

Rationality.

But near are these,
thoughts of doom.

So little effect...

Explosive eyes.
Kaleidoscope cries.

My demons cry sleeping.

Tamed no more.
Angry and sore.

Longing to,
break the chains.

To feel alive.

To rip free,
of collar once more.

To believe in days unseen.
To survive.

If only,
to avenge,
the capture.

{ The Valley of the Mind }

The valley of the mind,
withered;
chaotic...

Static charge flows,
as I walk through,
uneven uncertain surfaces.

Riddled with the craters,
of thoughts,
and teetering sanity.

Once rich and fulfilling...

New ideas molding,
every crevice,
of this valley.

Held down,
by foolish safeguards.

Mechanisms,
folded deep within,
mind's enigmatic matter.

Outdated witticisms,
coupled with molded,
moralities.

Reaching to the molten core,
of once pristine prism...

Hard contours full,
of redundant retardations,
of creativities.

Which are the past.

Supple and prolific.

Weeping willows abound.

Their tears,
clogging streams.

Formerly brilliant and clear.

Going down; defiling filth.

The stench of purity,
heart, and spirit.

Seething sexuality,
stifled by the oppressors.

A constant conflict of the masses.

The valley of the mind,
at war with,
the heart of the lamb.

Seeing mind controlled,
by the wasted dirt,
that is this world.

Observe its hills,
its boulders,
its ditches,
and its peaks.

Every crevice...

Filled with the mortar of untruth.

An adhesive with caustic properties,
purpose of detriment.

Sabotaging the spirit,
of valley rarely traveled.

But I must depart quickly!

Before it infests,
with its rot,
its filth,
its plague!

Too many unthought communications,
unthinkable.

Easily communicable,
herd mind mentality disease,
through contact.

Valley surface,
lays barren with doubt.

An ever present self loathing,
of who they believe...

We are supposed to be.

{ To Each Their Own }

To each their own,
in life and in death.

Countless spiderous paths,
in each garden,
of infinite decisions.

Variable.

To each their own,
in life and in death.

But may they choose wisely,
the ones who follow alongside,
so they do not,
piss upon,
roads ahead uncertain.

{ Gone Away }

One sliver of insanity,
reigns supreme.

A world alert,
so it would seem.

After all is gone and said.

Who or what,
will keep you,
holding on?

Time has gone away.
Dawn has struck its day.

When will you,
find time to play?

After time,
has left and gone away?

{ Thy Jaded Eyes }

I, tangled mess,
unraveled,
disheveled.

Where is my ending?

Where did I begin?

Life old-fashioned components,
self-serving patterns.

I did not like,
what I had become.

But my strings came undone,
more each day.

The stench of humanity,
deformed me.

I, delightfully ragged!

As I go,
I see,
my jaded eyes,
needed washing dirty...

Filth, a cleaning solution.

Get them,
out of my body,
out of my eyes,
out of my soul!

{ Halls of the Temple }

The halls of this temple,
they look so bleak.

The people are taken in,
they are so meek.

The music that resides here,
its rhythm and its rhyme.

It ensnares,
enfolds,
enslaves,
and transforms,
not by sound waves.

An existence of no liberty.
While seeing they are only led.

A flock,
led to a sordid trough.

Fed.

Living for souls,
only shells,
useless once dead.

{ Hallowed Ground }

The blood and pain,
trickles down thighs,
of worn cardboard.

After extinguished fireworks.
All this hallowed ground.
Just finished yet another eternity.

I am alive!
Am I dead inside?

Was there a bullet through my head?
Just fear of life?

Hindered and hoping.

Will I survive,
imminent descent,
toward ground below.

Does the time draw nigh,
for not even death releases fear.

Just a body finally alive,
frigid and faceless.

Only waiting to be buried.

{ The Fear of Tomorrow }

Walked in to silence,
of darkened room.

Looked at the things I could not see.

Their colors were beautiful.

Their depth gone,
the light was burned out.

Eyes of accusation,
cannot make themselves known,
in the dark.

Eyes of approval,
in the dark,
only see shapes.

Moving colors,
of grays and blacks.

The world of night,
a world of mystery misery.

The world of night.
The world of light.
They have one thing in common...

Judgment.
Boundaries.

Limitlessness.
No boundaries.

Everything impossible.
Anything is possible.

Nothing unreasonable.
Everything irrational.

Hemispheres colliding,
at dusk and at dawn,
bringing one breath,
into another...

Till all that was left,
was sweat, tears,
and the fear of tomorrow.

{ Beyond Pane }

Looked through,
windows of outside world.

I used to always gaze,
to the field beyond pane,
seeing beauty.

Those were childish times.

Times when,
I did not know,
what life could do...

Nostalgic remembering.
When those who used to come by here,
called themselves...

Friend.

Never again the times,
when we would frolic,
looking from place to place.

Never again,
one by one...

Watching them disappear.

Only a helpless spectator,
as erasures took place...

Never again,
the pain.

Every time I bring people in,
they disappear.

Solitude is the only solution.

{ Drowning in Dreams }

Flown away on a broken wing.
Started to fly only to sing.

Helping days and helping nights,
so many... drunken flights.

Dizzy and tired I fall,
asleep descending hard,
I begin to weep.

Holding my broken wings,
spread too far apart,
never mending wings,
of a broken heart.

Started too close to the sun,
but crashed into the deep.

Burning in flames.
Drowning in dreams.

Thankfully,
finally has come,
my final sleep.

{ The Valley of Happiness }

The world disappeared,
blinked out by the eyelid.

Its radiance slowly devoured,
by the ravenous appetites,
of the corrupt.

Torn now is the fabric,
of the great artwork.

A spoiled sunset,
in the valley of happiness

Restitched before rendered;
why try to resurrect a valley,
already barren and dead...

{ Destroyer of Dreams }

Always alone but never alone...

Everyone, please,
cast your first stone!

Wandering and waiting,
for the days to pass by.

Dead to the world,
flies consume my thigh.

Whispering words to hollow heads.
Waiting for bitter end of days.

Wondering when...
the whispering will stop.

Will mind stop?

Heartbroken,
too many times...

Just want to be,
be still my beating heart.

A beautiful horizontal line.

Kill this beating,
I call life.

Kill me with torn apart,
fabric of dreams.

I, the Alpha Omega.

Maker of dreams.
Destroyer of dreams!

The beginning.
The end?

Resurrection to murder.

True end search,
molten pains past.

Dead to the world,
eyes made of glass.

More dead inside,
every day.

1. for the dead.
2. for the glow.
3. your alive
4. it's time to go.

One day alone.
Two days have shown.
Three days dead and gone.
Four days forever alone...

{ Nightdream Horror Show }

Burned cold,
by love's caustic touch.

Grasping for a moment's serenity;
I was wishing for too much.

Patiently pondering night's cold;
ghost of strangers never really there.

Anticipatory gleam,
mouth's sorrowed slit.

Wilting away,
joyous memories,
bitter cold shit.

Groping for hope...

Nightdream wonderer,
still considering you.

Minutes caressing,
moments undressing,
meandering finding,
only charred ends.

Their pulse,
be it fate,
mind's eye passenger.

Bleak bitter road,
clouded by dust.

Howl forlorn.
Screech of delight.
Silent by destination.

Procrastination,
the icy highway on darkened night.

Muttering in anguish,
slumping broken life disease.

Yearning for a moment,
just seconds to please.

Drunk's sullen stare,
carries fingers fists.

Unrequited lust,
only a moment of weakness.

Brief moment.

Almost escaping...

Nightdream horror show.

Only silence left behind.

{ Pissed Away }

Last ditch efforts.
Suffering social lepers.

Deaf to the masses.

Working for pennies to save dollars.

Porn story masturbation,
only time she bothers.

Emotions like cigarettes,
eating away at compassion.

Only caring,
as part of the fashion.

Silken sheets,
covered in blood-stained forgiveness.

Happily ripping the dreams,
out of the hands of children.

Freedom burnt like charred bacon.

Pigs and governments are all the same;
all are dead
when someone plays that game.

Cold black heart of shame;
feeling and emotions do become feigned.

Left behind awake,
depressed days of broken sleep.

Simply,
a million dreams pissed away.

{ Private Matters }

Basking in guilty pleasures.
Mind flourishes with indulgence.
Sexual not sexual.

Flutters across mind's eye.

A brush meeting canvas.
Painting pictures of unrealities.

Forbidden dreams.
Do you call them guilty pleasures?

A bar of chocolate.
Another adultery?
All the same.

Murderous act: retribution
or abomination?

Lucifer in a sky with demons?

How can I see emeralds?
How do I see rubies?
How to break free of these diamonds?

I look to guilty pleasures.
I look to simple pleasures.
I look to innocent pleasures.

None suit my purpose;
break free from moral conquest.

Show gifts to yourself,
still they never do.

Why?

Because, they never embrace,

Themselves...

Dark places,
guilty places,
obscured by lies.

Afraid...

Better to show common face to
the adoring public;
self-loathing is a private matter.

{ Innocence }

Supple skin on tear stained sheets,
where innocence now lies beneath...

Blood fallen below,
heart still hammering.

Chastity gone.
Pale skin turned pink.

Flushed face,
where new knowledge seeps.

A fracture in time.
Innocence gone but not forgotten.

Eyes not soon spent,
time came and intruder went.

Breath was meek,
hands do hold her until one weeps.

Ghostly memories,
times anguish released.

Be still the bastion,
as one learns peace.

{ Pet Farm }

A golden farce started with,
a thrust and a grunt.

Feeling hymen burst...

Intrusion of mind burn blister skin.
Things cool. Start to shiver.

Worry sets in...

Ask yourself, did you give it
to an angel, a demon, or the Devil?

Did passion drain from your soul?
Was it ignited with the force?

Lust unabashed
within mind soul tonight.

End of beginning
begins with thrust of flesh...

Now, there's only
the future left for you.
Find yourself hidden
in passages of caress.

Expedient lustful undress.

Build the destruction
of your auto-pilot.
Trained by
society's withered quarrels...

Change brings heights
of new things to come...

Feeling fears change.

Thankfulness of wind thrown ashes,
of the robot you used to be.

Rising up of the forces,
that tried to pull you back,
from the beckoning unknown...

Seething carcasses once beautiful.

Care forgotten as rust sets in.

Following in droll mundane existence.

Society's robots,
the unlubricated pet farm.

Please, keep well oiled,
don't become the rusted cog.

It is time to care about every step,
or don't care at all.

Forget middle ground and...

Enjoy. Every. Moment.

{ Do Me Harm }

My head.

My hands.

My eyes.

My arms.

All trying to do me harm!

My taste.

My smell.

My touch.

My sight.

All saying I should die this night.

My lust.

My greed.

My sloth.

My vanity.

All making sure I will bleed!

My heart.

My mind.

My being.

My insanity.

All bringing blades
to my soul this night.

{ September 1939 }

Lightning strikes silently
in the night.
Burned earth still sparking...
Terminals of my mind...
Re-ignited;
ignited with spirit of renewal.
Thought dead long ago.
A plug had been pulled.
A circuit had broken.
By the flip of the switch
the diodes spark...
(I am alive again!)

Soon comes the hum of an old TV...
or maybe radio...

Turn crackling volume up.
Electricity surges!
Compression bulbs pop.
Coming to life again,
too many years of silence...
Old tunes playing in rewired head.
Volume rises again!
Again, I feel the electricity
in my veins.
These electron skirmish in my arteries.
Making mind feel alive again,
a mind not of the tempered sane.

Hearing voices muted in unison.
Watching as minutes and hours pass.
Wavering, tingling...
hearing the electricity in the air.

Feeling a tingle in wooden skin...
Feeling power flow,
once again pouring in.
Please,
take care not to trip over my cord.
This is an electric bill
I can absolutely not afford.
So don't say a word,
you may lose your breath.
One can't electrocute me,
it is my blood.
See the twinkle in my eyes?
Forgive me, forget me...
live in a flash, burn out in a moment.
Electronic, Electric... plug me in...
spirit in a flash is surely no sin.

{ The Everlasting Purgatory
of a Soul's Gentle Tune }

I now feel the clay beneath my fingers;
looking around at the gazing strangers.

I cry my tears.
Splashing down.
Rippling waters.

Creating mirrors from my mind.
Her face in time.

Clawing dirt.
I want her again.

In aquatic world,
frail body lost its oxygen.
Still, I found no release.
Now, my delicate love has joined the
deceased.

She left that warm summer's night.
Not a fear, nor a care.
She... encompassed with joy and
delight.

If only for a moment.
A glimmer in time...

Now you know the story;
tell no one my crime.

{ The Valley of Death Shadows }

I walk in the valley of death shadows.
I feel her presence in the air.
I smell the corpses.
(those she has taken the days before).
I walk with her as a friend.
I see her for what she is.

Not evil.
Not bad.

Only as one who transforms.

That which she does,
has been firmly established

Bringer of change,
none shall defeat her.

Not one passes her unwavering eye.
A valley we all must pass through.

The rich.
The poor.

All colors.
All social class.
All... everything.

Everywhere.

She sees no boundaries.
She feels no guilt.

Grim she is not!
Only reaping what she must!

A job is a job after all.

Why not make a livelihood,
out of the dead?

She rips us all to this valley,
where we walk,
when we walk.

The hills we climb must come to an end.
A valley's final curtain.

Rewards many and none.

Our journey has ended,
but, grim reaping goes on.

It is never done........

No one but grim can forever walk,
the valley of death shadows...

Honesty, the truest of all evils.

www.ingramcontent.com/pod-product-compliance
Lightning Source LLC
LaVergne TN
LVHW041315080426
835513LV00008B/469